A Guide to Gino Wickman's Book

WORKBOOK

Traction

The Get a Grip on Your Business

DISCLAIMER

We are delighted to present this companion workbook, thoughtfully crafted to complement and enrich your engagement with the insightful content found in 'Traction: Get a Grip on Your Business' by Gino Wickman. This workbook has been meticulously designed to elevate your comprehension and practical application of the concepts introduced in the original text, providing valuable assistance on your journey towards organizational success and effectiveness.

It is crucial to acknowledge that this supplementary workbook is intended to deepen your understanding of the fundamental material and is not meant to replace the primary text. Within these pages, you will find practical exercises, thoughtful prompts, and actionable activities inspired by the wisdom shared in 'Traction: Get a Grip on Your Business.' However, it is essential to recognize that this workbook does not serve as a substitute for a thorough exploration of the main book and its associated content.

We highly recommend obtaining the original source material, 'Traction: Get a Grip on Your Business' by Gino Wickman, to fully grasp the depth of insights and principles crucial for business growth. As you engage with the contents of this workbook, please keep in mind that its purpose is to reinforce and enhance the concepts introduced in the main text.

We are confident that this workbook will prove to be a valuable tool as you continue to delve into and solidify your understanding of the profound subject matter within 'Traction: Get a Grip on Your Business.' Your interaction with these transformative ideas for business improvement is further enhanced through this companion workbook, and we extend our best wishes for a fulfilling journey towards enhanced business success and achievement.

HOW TO USE THIS WORKBOOK

Welcome to the 'Traction: Get a Grip on Your Business' Companion Workbook! Here's a guide on how to effectively utilize this workbook alongside the original book by Gino Wickman:

- **Start with the Main Book:** Begin your exploration by reading the main source, 'Traction: Get a Grip on Your Business' by Gino Wickman. This foundational text introduces the core components and concepts that will be further explored and reinforced in this companion workbook.
- **Define Your Workbook Objectives:** Clearly outline your business goals and intentions. Whether you aim to enhance leadership, streamline processes, or foster a high-performing team, having clear objectives will help you tailor your engagement with the workbook effectively.
- **Follow the Workbook Structure:** This workbook is organized to complement the content of 'Traction: Get a Grip on Your Business.' Progress through the sections in the provided order, aligning with the book's six key components and strategies for business growth and success.
- **Participate in Practical Exercises:** Each section of the workbook contains practical exercises, thoughtful prompts, and actionable activities designed to facilitate practical application in your business. Set aside

dedicated time for these exercises to deepen your understanding of the book's principles.

- **Apply Concepts to Your Business:** Consider how the concepts can be integrated into your business operations. Identify practical ways to incorporate these principles into your daily routines, leadership strategies, and overall business development.
- **Refer to the Main Book:** Whenever the workbook refers to specific sections or concepts from 'Traction: Get a Grip on Your Business,' make sure to revisit the original source for a more comprehensive exploration. The workbook is intended to enhance your understanding but does not replace the main book.
- **Maintain a Workbook Journal:** Keep a journal to record your thoughts, reflections, and insights as you progress through the workbook. Your journal will serve as a valuable record of your business growth journey and as a source of motivation for ongoing improvement.
- **Engage in Discussions:** Foster meaningful discussions with your team, colleagues, or mentors about the concepts and strategies presented in 'Traction.' These conversations can offer new perspectives and deepen your understanding of the material.
- **Consistency is Key:** Set aside regular and focused time to work through the workbook. Consistency will help you internalize the principles and make them an integral part of your daily business routine and overall growth strategy.

- **Review and Revisit:** Periodically revisit your journal, notes, and completed workbook exercises. This practice will reinforce your learning and serve as a reminder of the progress you've made on your journey towards business success and achievement.

Remember, this workbook is designed to enhance your engagement with 'Traction: Get a Grip on Your Business' and its transformative insights into business management and growth. Your active participation and practical application of these principles will empower you to build a high-performing business. Embrace the journey towards business success as you explore the content within these pages.

Table Of Content

CHAPTER 1 The Entrepreneurial Operating System®: Strengthening the Six Key Components

CHAPTER SUMMARY

Chapter 1 of the Entrepreneurial Operating System (EOS) guide introduces the concept of strengthening the six key components of a business. The chapter begins by explaining that the EOS is a system designed to help entrepreneurs and business owners simplify their operations and achieve their goals.

The chapter then goes on to describe the six key components of the EOS, which are: vision, people, data, issues, process, and traction. The vision component involves creating a clear and compelling vision for the business, while the people component focuses on building a strong and cohesive team. The data component involves using data to make informed decisions, while the issues component involves identifying and solving problems in a systematic way. The process component involves documenting and improving key processes, while the traction component involves setting and achieving goals.

The chapter also introduces the concept of the Organizational Checkup, which is a tool that business owners can use to assess where their company is on the path to implementing the EOS. The checkup involves answering a series of questions about each of the six key components, and then using a key to interpret the results.

Finally, the chapter discusses the importance of letting go of bad habits and unhealthy practices that may be holding a business back. This is referred to as "letting go of the vine," and is seen as a necessary step in implementing the EOS.

Overall, Chapter 1 provides an overview of the EOS system and introduces the six key components that will be explored in more detail in subsequent chapters. It emphasizes the importance of having a clear vision, building a strong team, using data to make informed decisions, and setting and achieving goals.

SELF REFLECTION QUESTIONS

How clear is my business vision, and how effectively am I communicating it to my team? What steps can I take to improve my vision and ensure that everyone is aligned with it?

How strong is my team, and what can I do to build a more cohesive and effective team? Are there any skills or training opportunities that would benefit my team members?

How well am I using data to make informed decisions in my business? Are there any areas where I could improve my data collection or analysis processes?

What bad habits or practices am I holding onto that may be holding my business back? How can I identify and let go of these habits to create space for growth and improvement?

ACTION PROMPTS

1. Assess your business's current state: Use the Organizational Checkup tool provided in the chapter to assess where your business stands in terms of the six key components of the EOS. This will help you identify areas that need improvement and set priorities for implementing the system.

2. Define your business vision: Take the time to create a clear and compelling vision for your business that can be communicated to your team. This will help ensure that everyone is working towards the same goals and will make it easier to make decisions that align with your vision.

3. Build a strong team: Focus on building a cohesive team that is aligned with your vision and values. This may involve hiring new team members, providing training and development opportunities, and creating a culture that fosters collaboration and accountability.

4. Let go of bad habits: Identify any unhealthy practices or habits that may be holding your business back and commit to letting them go. This may involve delegating tasks to others, adopting new processes and systems, or simply changing the way you approach certain tasks or decisions. By letting go of the vine, you can create space for new growth and improvement.

CHAPTER 2 Letting Go of the Vine

CHAPTER SUMMARY

Chapter 2 of the book is titled "Letting Go of the Vine" and focuses on the importance of taking a leap of faith in order to grow your business. The chapter begins by discussing the common reasons why business owners struggle to let go of the vine, such as fear of failure, lack of trust in others, and the belief that they are the only ones who can do things right.

The chapter then introduces the EOS (Entrepreneurial Operating System) tools that can help business owners overcome these challenges and let go of the vine. These tools include the Vision/Traction Organizer, which helps businesses clarify their vision and set goals, and the Accountability Chart, which helps businesses define roles and responsibilities and ensure everyone is working towards the same goals.

The chapter also emphasizes the importance of taking action and not getting stuck in analysis paralysis. It encourages business owners to trust the EOS process and take a leap of faith, even if it feels uncomfortable or scary. The chapter provides examples of how the EOS process has helped other businesses grow, such as increasing revenue, improving employee engagement, and streamlining operations.

Overall, Chapter 2 of the book is a call to action for business owners to let go of the vine and take a leap of faith in order to grow their businesses. It provides practical tools and examples to help business owners overcome their fears and trust the EOS process.

SELF REFLECTION QUESTIONS

What are some common reasons why business owners struggle to let go of the vine, and how can these challenges be overcome using the EOS tools discussed in Chapter 2?

How can the Vision/Traction Organizer and Accountability Chart help businesses clarify their vision, set goals, and ensure everyone is working towards the same goals?

What are some examples of how the EOS process has helped other businesses grow, and how can these success stories inspire and motivate business owners to take a leap of faith?

How can business owners overcome analysis paralysis and take action to grow their businesses, even if it feels uncomfortable or scary? What are some practical steps they can take to trust the EOS process and let go of the vine?

ACTION PROMPTS

1. Use the Vision/Traction Organizer to clarify your business's vision and set specific, measurable goals for growth. Identify any fears or challenges that may be holding you back from taking action, and brainstorm ways to overcome these obstacles using the EOS tools discussed in Chapter 2.

2. Create an Accountability Chart that clearly defines roles and responsibilities for everyone in your organization. Use this chart to ensure everyone is working towards the same goals and to identify any areas where additional support or resources may be needed.

3. Take a leap of faith and trust the EOS process, even if it feels uncomfortable or scary. Remember that hitting the

ceiling is inevitable, and that letting go of the vine is necessary for growth. Use the practical tools and examples provided in Chapter 2 to inspire and motivate you to take action.

4. Don't get stuck in analysis paralysis - take action to grow your business today. Identify one specific step you can take right now to move your business forward, whether it's delegating a task to a team member, setting a new goal, or scheduling a meeting to discuss your vision and priorities. Remember that small steps can lead to big results over time.

CHAPTER 3 The Vision Component: Do They See What You Are Saying?

CHAPTER SUMMARY

Chapter 3 of the book is titled "The Vision Component" and focuses on the importance of clarifying and effectively communicating your vision to your team. The chapter begins by emphasizing the need for entrepreneurs to get their vision out of their heads and onto paper. This is because a clear and well-defined vision can help guide decision-making, inspire and motivate team members, and ultimately lead to the success of the organization.

The chapter then goes on to discuss the process of creating a three-year picture, which involves identifying key factors such as resources, office environment, operational efficiencies, technology needs, product mix, and client mix. After some discussion and debate, the leadership team should come up with 10 to 20 bullet points that describe what the organization will look like in three years. Each person on the team should also verbalize their vision for their individual role in the organization during that time frame.

Once the three-year picture has been created, it is important to ensure that everyone on the leadership team sees it clearly. This can be done by having everyone close their eyes as one person reads the picture out loud. The picture must be visible in each person's mind, and each person must believe in it and ultimately want it. The team should be encouraged to speak up, debate, and go back and forth, but ultimately they must agree on all of the major points.

The chapter also discusses the importance of effectively communicating the vision to the rest of the organization. This can be done through a variety of methods, such as town hall meetings, one-on-one conversations, and written materials. It is important to ensure that everyone in the organization understands the vision and how their role contributes to its realization.

Finally, the chapter highlights some common mistakes that entrepreneurs make when it comes to sharing their vision with their organization. These include not being clear and specific enough, not communicating the vision frequently enough, and not involving team members in the process of creating the vision.

Overall, Chapter 3 emphasizes the importance of having a clear and well-defined vision, and provides practical advice on how to create and communicate that vision effectively. By doing so, entrepreneurs can inspire and motivate their team members, and ultimately lead their organization to success.

SELF REFLECTION QUESTIONS

How can creating a three-year picture help guide decision-making and motivate team members?

What are some effective methods for communicating a vision to the rest of the organization, and why is it important to ensure that everyone understands the vision?

What are some common mistakes that entrepreneurs make when it comes to sharing their vision with their organization, and how can these mistakes be avoided?

How can involving team members in the process of creating a vision help ensure that everyone is on board and committed to its realization?

ACTION PROMPTS

1. Schedule a leadership team meeting to create a three-year picture for your organization. Identify key factors such as resources, office environment, operational efficiencies, technology needs, product mix, and client mix, and come up with 10 to 20 bullet points that describe what the organization will look like in three years.

2. Develop a plan for effectively communicating your vision to the rest of the organization. Consider methods such as town hall meetings, one-on-one conversations, and written materials, and ensure that everyone in the organization understands the vision and how their role contributes to its realization.

3. Reflect on common mistakes that entrepreneurs make when it comes to sharing their vision with their organization, such as not being clear and specific enough, not communicating the vision frequently enough, and not involving team members in the process of creating the vision. Identify ways to avoid these mistakes in your own organization.

4. Involve team members in the process of creating a vision for your organization. Encourage open discussion and debate, and ensure that everyone on the team sees the vision clearly and believes in it. This can help ensure that everyone is on board and committed to its realization.

CHAPTER 4 The People Component: Surround Yourself with Good People

CHAPTER SUMMARY

Chapter 4 of the book is titled "The People Component" and focuses on the importance of surrounding yourself with good people and getting the right people in the right seats. The chapter begins by discussing how great leaders frequently credit their success to having "good people," but what exactly does that mean? The author explains that it's about identifying individuals who share your company's core values and fit into your culture, making your organization a better place to be.

The chapter then goes on to discuss the importance of getting the right people in the right seats. This means finding individuals who are not only a good fit for your company culture but also have the skills and experience necessary to excel in their roles. The author emphasizes that it's not just about filling positions but about finding the right people for those positions.

To help with this process, the author introduces the People Analyzer, a tool that can be used in quarterly performance reviews with all team members. The People Analyzer helps identify individuals who are a good fit for your company culture and those who may not be. It also helps identify areas where team members may need additional training or support.

The chapter concludes by discussing the importance of creating a culture that attracts and retains good people. This means creating an environment where individuals feel valued, supported, and challenged. The author emphasizes that this is not just about offering perks or benefits but about creating a culture that aligns with your company's core values and mission.

Overall, Chapter 4 of the book emphasizes the importance of getting the right people in the right seats and creating a culture that attracts and retains good people. The People Analyzer is introduced as a tool to help with this process, and the author provides tips and strategies for creating a culture that aligns with your company's core values and mission.

SELF REFLECTION QUESTIONS

How can I identify individuals who share my company's core values and fit into my organization's culture?

What strategies can I use to ensure that I am getting the right people in the right seats within my organization?

How can I use the People Analyzer tool to identify areas where team members may need additional training or support?

 What steps can I take to create a culture that aligns with my company's core values and mission, and attracts and retains good people?

ACTION PROMPTS

1. Conduct a review of your company's core values and mission statement to ensure that they are clearly defined and communicated to all team members.

2. Use the People Analyzer tool to conduct quarterly performance reviews with all team members, and identify areas where additional training or support may be needed.

3. Develop a hiring process that focuses on finding individuals who not only have the necessary skills and

experience but also share your company's core values and fit into your culture.

4. Create a culture that aligns with your company's core values and mission by offering opportunities for growth and development, recognizing and rewarding good performance, and fostering open communication and collaboration among team members.

CHAPTER 5 The Data Component: Safety in Numbers

CHAPTER SUMMARY

Chapter 5 of the book is titled "The Data Component: Safety in Numbers." This chapter emphasizes the importance of data in managing a business and provides a framework for collecting and analyzing data effectively.

The chapter begins by painting a picture of a small plane flying over the Atlantic Ocean, with the captain announcing that the gauges aren't working and they are hopelessly lost. This scenario serves as a metaphor for the dangers of managing a business without accurate and consistent data.

The chapter then introduces the concept of a scorecard, which is a time-tested tool for quantifying a company's results. The scorecard allows business owners to monitor their business on a weekly basis and quickly identify which activities are on track or off track. By tracking these numbers over time, business owners can identify patterns and trends and make predictions about the future.

The chapter emphasizes the importance of having a chosen handful of numbers to monitor, rather than trying to track every possible metric. This allows business owners to focus on the most important aspects of their business and avoid getting bogged down in irrelevant details.

The chapter also discusses the importance of assigning numbers to every member of the organization, giving them clear direction and increasing productivity. This approach helps to create a culture of accountability and ensures that everyone is working towards the same goals.

The chapter concludes by emphasizing the power of data to help business owners make effective decisions and sleep better at night. By letting go of subjective opinions and assumptions and relying on hard data, business owners can manage their business with confidence and achieve greater success.

SELF REFLECTION QUESTIONS

How can I identify the most important metrics to track in my business, and how can I use these metrics to monitor my business on a weekly basis?

How can I create a culture of accountability in my organization by assigning numbers to every member of the team, and how can this approach increase productivity?

What are some common mistakes to avoid when using data to make decisions, and how can I ensure that I am relying on accurate and consistent information?

How can I use the scorecard tool to identify patterns and trends in my business, and how can I use this information to make predictions about the future?

ACTION PROMPTS

1. Identify the most important metrics for your business and create a scorecard to track these metrics on a weekly basis. Use this information to monitor your business and make data-driven decisions.

2. Assign numbers to every member of your organization and use these numbers to create a culture of accountability. This will help to ensure that everyone is working towards the same goals and increase productivity.

3. Avoid common mistakes when using data to make decisions, such as relying on subjective opinions and assumptions. Instead, focus on hard data and ensure that you are using accurate and consistent information.

4. Use the scorecard tool to identify patterns and trends in your business, and use this information to make predictions about the future. This will help you to stay ahead of the curve and make proactive decisions to drive your business forward.

CHAPTER 6 The Issues Component: Decide!

CHAPTER SUMMARY

Chapter 6 of the book focuses on the "Issues Component" of the Entrepreneurial Operating System (EOS). The chapter emphasizes the importance of facing and solving issues as they arise in order to achieve greater success and growth for an organization.

The chapter begins by discussing the common reasons why organizations struggle to solve issues, including a lack of transparency, accountability, and discipline. The author notes that many companies tend to avoid or ignore problems, which can lead to bigger issues down the line.

To address these challenges, the chapter introduces the EOS process for solving issues. This process involves identifying and prioritizing issues, discussing potential solutions, and then making a decision on how to move forward. The chapter provides a detailed breakdown of each step in the process, including tips for facilitating productive discussions and making effective decisions.

One key takeaway from the chapter is the importance of taking action and making decisions, even if they are not perfect. The author notes that indecision can be more damaging than making the wrong decision, and that successful companies are those that are able to quickly and efficiently solve problems.

Throughout the chapter, the author provides real-world examples of companies that have successfully implemented the discipline of solving issues. These examples illustrate how the EOS process can help create a culture of transparency and accountability within an organization, leading to greater success and growth.

Overall, Chapter 6 of the book provides a comprehensive overview of the Issues Component of the EOS, emphasizing the importance of facing and solving problems in order to achieve success and growth for an organization. The chapter provides practical tips and real-world examples to help readers implement the EOS process in their own organizations.

SELF REFLECTION QUESTIONS

How can your organization improve its approach to problem-solving and decision-making? What steps can you take to create a culture of transparency and accountability, and ensure that issues are addressed quickly and efficiently?

What are some common challenges that organizations face when it comes to solving issues? How can you overcome these challenges and create a more effective problem-solving process?

How can you prioritize issues and ensure that the most important problems are addressed first? What criteria should you use to determine which issues require immediate attention, and which can be addressed later?

How can you encourage your team to take action and make decisions, even if they are not perfect? What strategies can you use to overcome indecision and ensure that your organization is moving forward and making progress?

ACTION PROMPTS

1. Create a list of the most pressing issues facing your organization, and prioritize them based on their impact and urgency. Use the EOS process for solving issues to address each problem systematically, and ensure that each issue is resolved before moving on to the next.

2. Establish a culture of transparency and accountability within your organization by encouraging open communication and feedback. Create a safe space for team members to share their concerns and ideas, and ensure that everyone is held accountable for their actions and decisions.

3. Develop a set of criteria for making decisions, and use these criteria to guide your team's decision-making process. Consider factors such as impact, feasibility, and alignment with your organization's goals and values.

4. Encourage your team to take action and make decisions, even if they are not perfect. Emphasize the importance of learning from mistakes and using failures as opportunities for growth and improvement. Celebrate successes and milestones along the way to keep your team motivated and engaged.

CHAPTER 7 The Process Component: Finding Your Way

CHAPTER SUMMARY

Chapter 7 of the book focuses on the Process Component and its importance in building a successful business. The chapter begins with a quote from Jim Weichert, the founder of Weichert, Realtors, who attributes his company's success to consistency. The chapter then goes on to explain how consistency can be achieved through the implementation of core processes.

The chapter emphasizes the need for entrepreneurs to identify and document their core processes in order to create efficiencies and simplify their operations. By doing so, they can ensure that their business is self-sustaining and can run without them. The chapter provides a step-by-step guide for identifying and documenting core processes, which includes reviewing the People Analyzer, documenting the review, and filing it with the HR department.

The chapter also discusses the importance of packaging core processes once they have been documented. This involves creating a table of contents using the titles of the core processes and organizing the documented processes into sections. The chapter notes that each core process will typically run between two and ten pages, with operations processes being the longest.

The chapter cautions entrepreneurs not to be too constricted by the 20/80 rule and to include whatever they feel is necessary. However, they should keep it simple and avoid unnecessary steps that may have been put in place simply because "we've always done it that way."

The chapter concludes by emphasizing the importance of consistency and the Process Component in building a successful business. It notes that by understanding and implementing core processes, entrepreneurs can improve efficiency, save time, and increase control. The chapter encourages entrepreneurs not to neglect this crucial component of their organization.

SELF REFLECTION QUESTIONS

What are the core processes that make up my unique business model, and how can I ensure that everyone in my organization understands and follows them?

How can I take a high-level view of my organization from time to time to appreciate what has been built and identify areas for improvement?

What are some common mistakes that entrepreneurs make when it comes to the Process Component, and how can I avoid them in my own business?

How can I clarify and hone my systems to run my business, rather than having my business run me? What steps can I take to ensure that my business is self-sustaining and can run without me?

ACTION PROMPTS

1. Identify the core processes that make up your unique business model and document them in a clear and concise manner. Use the step-by-step guide provided in the chapter to review and document your processes, and file them with your HR department for easy access.

2. Take a high-level view of your organization from time to time to appreciate what has been built and identify areas for improvement. Use this perspective to identify inefficiencies and streamline your processes.

3. Avoid common mistakes that entrepreneurs make when it comes to the Process Component by keeping your

processes simple and avoiding unnecessary steps. Focus on creating efficiencies and simplification, rather than hype.

4. Clarify and hone your systems to run your business, rather than having your business run you. Ensure that your business is self-sustaining and can run without you by getting your key processes out of your head and onto paper. This will allow someone to step in and pick up right where you left off if something were to happen to you or any of your people.

CHAPTER 8 The Traction Component: From Luftmensch to Action!

CHAPTER SUMMARY

Chapter 8 of the book is titled "The Traction Component: From Luftmensch to Action!" and focuses on the process of turning a vision into reality and gaining traction within an organization. The chapter begins by emphasizing the importance of taking action and making progress towards goals, rather than simply talking about them.

The author notes that in order to gain traction, several key components must be in place, including a clear vision, the right people in the right seats, effective data management, a process for solving issues, and a defined Way of doing business. These components are discussed in detail in earlier chapters of the guide.

The chapter then goes on to discuss the importance of accountability and discipline in gaining traction. The author notes that successful leaders rate themselves high in accountability and that organizations with strong accountability and discipline are more likely to achieve their goals. The author provides several tips for improving accountability and discipline, including setting clear expectations, establishing consequences for not meeting expectations, and regularly reviewing progress towards goals.

The chapter also discusses the importance of having a system for tracking progress and holding people accountable. The author recommends using a scorecard to track key metrics and ensure that everyone is aligned and working towards the same goals. The chapter concludes by emphasizing the importance of taking action and making progress towards goals, rather than simply talking about them, and notes that gaining traction requires discipline, accountability, and a commitment to continuous improvement.

SELF REFLECTION QUESTIONS

How can I ensure that I have the right people in the right seats to gain traction within my organization?

What steps can I take to improve accountability and discipline within my organization, and how can I ensure that everyone is aligned and working towards the same goals?

How can I establish a system for tracking progress and holding people accountable, and what metrics should I be tracking to ensure that we are making progress towards our goals?

What steps can I take to ensure that I am taking action and making progress towards my goals, rather than simply talking about them, and how can I maintain discipline and accountability over the long term?

ACTION PROMPTS

1. Review your organization's vision and ensure that it is clear and well-defined. Identify any gaps in your current approach and develop a plan to address them.

2. Evaluate your organization's accountability and discipline levels and identify areas for improvement. Develop a plan to establish clear expectations, consequences, and regular progress reviews.

3. Establish a system for tracking progress towards your goals, such as a scorecard or dashboard. Identify key metrics to track and ensure that everyone is aligned and working towards the same goals.

4. Commit to taking action and making progress towards your goals, rather than simply talking about them. Develop a plan to maintain discipline and accountability over the long term, and regularly review progress towards your goals to ensure that you are on track.

CHAPTER 9 Pulling It All Together: The Grand Journey

CHAPTER SUMMARY

Chapter 9 of the book "Pulling It All Together: The Grand Journey" is the final chapter of the guide and provides a comprehensive summary of the Entrepreneurial Operating System (EOS) model. The chapter aims to help readers understand how to implement the Six Key Components of the EOS model to achieve 100% success in running their organization.

The chapter begins by summarizing the Six Key Components of the EOS model, which include Vision, People, Data, Issues, Process, and Traction. The author explains that these components are interconnected and that strengthening each component can help build a great organization and reduce frustrations.

The chapter then goes on to provide a detailed explanation of each component. The Vision Component is about creating a clear and compelling vision for the organization that everyone can understand and get behind. The People Component is about getting the right people in the right seats and creating a healthy and cohesive team. The Data Component is about using data to make informed decisions and track progress. The Issues Component is about identifying and solving problems quickly and effectively. The Process Component is about creating a consistent way of doing things that everyone can follow. Finally, the Traction Component is about executing on the vision and achieving measurable results.

The author emphasizes that implementing the EOS model is not a one-time event but an ongoing process. He provides a step-by-step guide on how to implement the EOS model, which includes identifying the right people to lead the process, creating a clear vision, getting everyone on the same page, and implementing the Six Key Components.

The chapter concludes by emphasizing the importance of staying focused on the journey and not just the results. The author encourages readers to embrace the journey-focused approach and fight society's pull towards rewarding results over processes. He reminds readers that staying focused is the key to happiness and success.

In summary, Chapter 9 "Pulling It All Together: The Grand Journey" provides a comprehensive summary of the Entrepreneurial Operating System (EOS) model. The chapter explains the Six Key Components of the EOS model and provides a step-by-step guide on how to implement the model. The author emphasizes the importance of staying focused on the journey and not just the results and encourages readers to embrace the journey-focused approach.

SELF REFLECTION QUESTIONS

How can implementing the Six Key Components of the Entrepreneurial Operating System (EOS) model help me build a great organization and reduce my frustrations?

What are the steps involved in implementing the EOS model, and how can I ensure that I have the right people to lead the process?

How can I create a clear and compelling vision for my organization that everyone can understand and get behind?

How can I stay focused on the journey and not just the results, and what are some strategies I can use to fight society's pull towards rewarding results over processes?

ACTION PROMPTS

1. Identify the Six Key Components of the Entrepreneurial Operating System (EOS) model and assess how well your organization is currently performing in each area. Develop a plan to strengthen each component as needed.

2. Create a clear and compelling vision for your organization that everyone can understand and get behind. Communicate this vision to your team and ensure that everyone is on the same page.

3. Implement a consistent way of doing things that everyone can follow. This will help create a cohesive team and ensure that everyone is working towards the same goals.

4. Stay focused on the journey and not just the results. Embrace the journey-focused approach and develop strategies to fight society's pull towards rewarding results over processes. Celebrate small wins along the way and use them as motivation to keep moving forward.

CHAPTER 10 Getting Started

CHAPTER SUMMARY

Chapter 10 of the book is titled "Getting Started" and provides a comprehensive guide on how to implement the Entrepreneurial Operating System (EOS) tools in the most efficient way possible. The chapter begins by introducing the EOS Model, which is a holistic framework that helps businesses achieve their goals by strengthening the Six Key Components of their organization. These components include Vision, People, Data, Issues, Process, and Traction.

The chapter then goes on to explain the importance of implementing the EOS tools in the right order. The recommended sequence is as follows: Vision, People, Data, Issues, Process, and Traction. The reason for this order is that each tool builds on the previous one, and implementing them in the right sequence ensures that the organization is ready for the next tool.

The chapter then provides a detailed explanation of each tool, including its purpose, how to implement it, and what results to expect. For example, the Vision tool helps businesses clarify their long-term goals and create a shared vision that everyone in the organization can work towards. The People tool helps businesses identify the right people for the right seats, and create an accountability chart that clarifies everyone's roles and responsibilities.

The chapter also provides tips on how to get the most out of each tool, such as involving everyone in the organization in the implementation process, setting clear goals and timelines, and holding regular check-ins to ensure that progress is being made.

Finally, the chapter provides real-world examples of companies that have successfully implemented the EOS tools and achieved significant results. For example, one company was able to increase its revenue by 50% and reduce its employee turnover rate by 80% after implementing the EOS tools.

Overall, Chapter 10 of the book provides a comprehensive guide on how to implement the EOS tools in the most efficient way possible, and how to get the most out of each tool. By following the recommended sequence and tips provided in this chapter, businesses can strengthen the Six Key Components of their organization and achieve their long-term goals.

SELF REFLECTION QUESTIONS

How can implementing the EOS tools in the recommended sequence help businesses achieve their long-term goals more efficiently?

What are some of the key benefits of using the EOS Model to strengthen the Six Key Components of an organization?

How can involving everyone in the organization in the implementation process help ensure that the EOS tools are successful?

What are some of the real-world examples of companies that have successfully implemented the EOS tools, and what can we learn from their experiences?

ACTION PROMPTS

1. Create a plan to implement the EOS tools in the recommended sequence, starting with the Vision tool. Set clear goals and timelines for each tool, and involve everyone in the organization in the implementation process.

2. Use the People tool to identify the right people for the right seats in your organization. Create an accountability chart that clarifies everyone's roles and responsibilities, and hold regular check-ins to ensure that everyone is on track.

3. Develop a Scorecard that measures the right activity-based numbers and clearly identifies the person who ultimately owns each number. Use this tool to create real accountability and track progress towards your long-term goals.

4. Look for real-world examples of companies that have successfully implemented the EOS tools, and learn from their experiences. Identify what worked well for them and how you can apply those lessons to your own organization.

Made in United States
Orlando, FL
01 March 2025

59043466R00036